ABCs
of the Bible
Coloring Fun from A to Z

Illustrated by

Dan Sharp
Editor: Carol Layton
Layout Design: Mark Conrad
Cover Design: Peggy Jackson

Carson-Dellosa Publishing, LLC
Greensboro, North Carolina

Printed in the USA • All rights reserved.

ISBN: 978-0-88724-214-4

05-156181151

A is for Angel

He has put his angels in charge of you. They will
watch over you wherever you go. Psalm 91:11 (ICB)

B is for **Bible**

God's word is alive and working. It is sharper than
a sword sharpened on both sides. Hebrews 4:12 (ICB)

C is for Cross

With the cross God won the victory. . . . Colossians 2:15 (ICB)

D is for Donkey

"Hosanna! . . . see, your king is coming, seated on a donkey's colt." John 12:13–15

E is for **Eve**

Adam named his wife Eve, because she would become the mother of all the living.
Genesis 3:20

6

F is for **Family**

"As for me and my family, we will serve the Lord."
Joshua 24:15 (ICB)

G is for **Goliath**

So David defeated the Philistine [Goliath] with only a sling and a stone!
1 Samuel 17:50 (ICB)

H is for Hymn

Speak to one another with psalms, hymns and spiritual songs. Ephesians 5:19

is for **Isaac**

Abraham gave the name Isaac to the son Sarah bore him. Genesis 21:3

J is for **Jesus**

God makes people right with himself through their faith in Jesus Christ.
Romans 3:22 (ICB)

K is for King David

And David knew that the Lᴏʀᴅ had established him as king over Israel. . . .
2 Samuel 5:12

12

L is for **Lamb**

You were bought with the precious blood of the death of Christ, who was like a pure and perfect lamb. 1 Peter 1:19 (ICB)

 CD-2028 *ABCs of the Bible*

M is for **Manger**

So they hurried off and found Mary and Joseph,
and the baby, who was lying in the manger. Luke 2:16

N is for **Noah**

The LORD then said to Noah, "Go into the ark, you and your whole family. . . ." Genesis 7:1

O is for **Offering**

Ascribe to the LORD the glory due his name;
bring an offering and come into his courts. Psalm 96:8

P is for **Parable**

Then he told them many things in parables, saying:
"A farmer went out to sow his seed." Matthew 13:3

Q is for **Queen of Sheba**

When the queen of Sheba saw all the wisdom of Solomon and the palace he had built . . . she was overwhelmed. 1 Kings 10:4-5

R is for **Rainbow**

I have set my rainbow in the clouds, and it will be the sign of the covenant between me and the earth. Genesis 9:13

S is for **Samuel**

Then all Israel, from Dan to Beersheba, knew Samuel was a prophet of the Lord.

1 Samuel 3:20 (ICB)

T is for **Ten Commandments**

And [Moses] wrote on the tablets the words of
the covenant—the Ten Commandments. Exodus 34:28

U is for **Unleavened Bread**

"Celebrate the Feast of Unleavened Bread, because it was on this very day that I brought your divisions out of Egypt." Exodus 12:17

V is for **Vine**

"I am the vine, and you are the branches. If a person remains in me and I remain in him, then he produces much fruit." John 15:5 (ICB)

W is for **Water**

Then they saw Jesus walking on the water, coming toward the boat. John 6:19 (ICB)

X is for **Xerxes**

So [King Xerxes] set a royal crown on her head and made [Esther] queen instead of Vashti. Esther 2:17

CD-2028 *ABCs of the Bible*

Y is for Yoke

Do not be yoked together with unbelievers. 2 Corinthians 6:14

Z is for Zaccheus

When Jesus reached the spot, he looked up and said to him, "Zacchaeus, come down immediately. I must stay at your house today." Luke 19:5

Suggestions for Using Scripture Cards

Play the following games by making two copies of the Scripture cards (pages 28–32) for each pair of players. Allow children to color the illustrations with colored pencils, if desired. Cut out the cards and laminate for durability.

- **Go Fish** Shuffle the two sets of cards and give five cards to each player. Each child takes a turn asking the other player for a card he is holding until all of the cards are matched. A player draws from the deck if his opponent doesn't have the requested card. Players draw more cards when they run out. When all of the cards are matched, players can separate the cards and then place them in alphabetical order.
- **Concentration** Shuffle the two sets of cards and place each card facedown. Have children take turns turning over two cards at a time until all of the cards have been matched.
- **ABC Race** Time individual children or let pairs of children race to put the Scripture cards in alphabetical order.
- **Memory Verse Flash Cards** (This requires only one set of cards per pair.) Write the letter and the word on the back of each photocopied card (for example, A is for Angel). Show the back of the card to a child to prompt her to recite the verse that goes with that letter.

A is for **Angel**

He has put his angels in charge of you.
They will watch over you wherever you go.
Psalm 91:11 (ICB)

B is for **Bible**

God's word is alive and working.
It is sharper than a sword sharpened
on both sides. Hebrews 4:12 (ICB)

C is for Cross

With the cross God won the victory. . . .
Colossians 2:15 (ICB)

D is for Donkey

"Hosanna! . . . see, your king is coming,
seated on a donkey's colt." John 12:13–15

E is for Eve

Adam named his wife Eve, because she would
become the mother of all the living. Genesis 3:20

F is for Family

"As for me and my family, we will
serve the Lord." Joshua 24:15 (ICB)

G is for Goliath

So David defeated the Philistine
[Goliath] with only a sling and a stone!
1 Samuel 17:50 (ICB)

H is for Hymn

Speak to one another with psalms, hymns
and spiritual songs. Ephesians 5:19

CD-2028 *ABCs of the Bible*

I is for Isaac

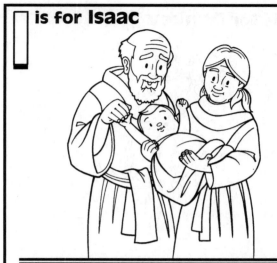

Abraham gave the name Isaac to the son Sarah bore him. Genesis 21:3

J is for Jesus

God makes people right with himself through their faith in Jesus Christ. Romans 3:22 (ICB)

K is for King David

And David knew that the Lord had established him as king over Israel. . . . 2 Samuel 5:12

L is for Lamb

You were bought with the precious blood of the death of Christ, who was like a pure and perfect lamb. 1 Peter 1:19 (ICB)

M is for Manger

So they hurried off and found Mary and Joseph, and the baby, who was lying in the manger. Luke 2:16

N is for Noah

The Lord then said to Noah, "Go into the ark, you and your whole family. . . ." Genesis 7:1

O is for **Offering**

Ascribe to the LORD the glory due his name;
bring an offering and come into his courts.
Psalm 96:8

P is for **Parable**

Then he told them many things in parables,
saying: "A farmer went out to sow his seed."
Matthew 13:3

Q is for **Queen of Sheba**

When the queen of Sheba saw all the
wisdom of Solomon and the palace he had
built . . . she was overwhelmed. 1 Kings 10:4–5

R is for **Rainbow**

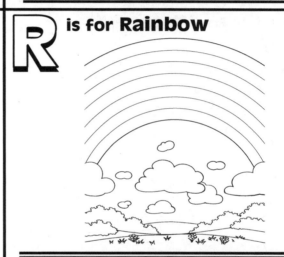

I have set my rainbow in the clouds,
and it will be the sign of the covenant
between me and the earth. Genesis 9:13

S is for **Samuel**

Then all Israel, from Dan to Beersheba,
knew Samuel was a prophet of the Lord.
1 Samuel 3:20 (ICB)

T is for **Ten Commandments**

And [Moses] wrote on the tablets the words
of the covenant—the Ten Commandments.
Exodus 34:28

U 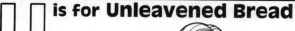 is for **Unleavened Bread**

"Celebrate the Feast of Unleavened Bread, because it was on this very day that I brought your divisions out of Egypt."
Exodus 12:17

V is for **Vine**

"I am the vine, and you are the branches. If a person remains in me and I remain in him, then he produces much fruit." John 15:5 (ICB)

W is for **Water**

Then they saw Jesus walking on the water, coming toward the boat. John 6:19 (ICB)

X is for **Xerxes**

So [King Xerxes] set a royal crown on her head and made [Esther] queen instead of Vashti. Esther 2:17

Y is for **Yoke**

Do not be yoked together with unbelievers.
2 Corinthians 6:14

Z is for **Zacchaeus**

When Jesus reached the spot, he looked up and said to him, "Zacchaeus, come down immediately. I must stay at your house today."
Luke 19:5